45 Blueberry Recipes for Home

By: Kelly Johnson

Table of Contents

- Classic Blueberry Pie
- Blueberry Muffins
- Blueberry Pancakes
- Blueberry Smoothie
- Blueberry Cheesecake
- Blueberry Jam
- Blueberry Scones
- Blueberry Cobbler
- Blueberry Lemonade
- Blueberry Ice Cream
- Blueberry Crisp
- Blueberry Banana Bread
- Blueberry Oatmeal Bars
- Blueberry Parfait
- Blueberry Breakfast Casserole
- Blueberry Vinaigrette Salad
- Blueberry Cheesecake Bars
- Blueberry and Almond Granola
- Blueberry Glazed Salmon
- Blueberry Greek Yogurt Popsicles
- Blueberry Almond Cake
- Blueberry BBQ Sauce
- Blueberry Shortcake
- Blueberry and Goat Cheese Salad
- Blueberry Lemon Loaf
- Blueberry Balsamic Chicken
- Blueberry Spinach Salad
- Blueberry and Ricotta Pancakes
- Blueberry Basil Lemonade
- Blueberry Cinnamon Rolls
- Blueberry Crumble Bars
- Blueberry and Feta Stuffed Chicken Breast
- Blueberry Whipped Cream
- Blueberry and Peach Sangria
- Blueberry Oatmeal Cookies

- Blueberry and Lemon Sorbet
- Blueberry and Walnut Bread
- Blueberry and Cream Cheese Stuffed French Toast Casserole
- Blueberry and Pecan Quinoa Salad
- Blueberry and Nutella Crepes
- Blueberry Basil Chicken
- Blueberry Pistachio Energy Bites
- Blueberry and Spinach Stuffed Salmon
- Blueberry and Balsamic Bruschetta
- Blueberry Tiramisu

Classic Blueberry Pie

Ingredients:

For the Pie Crust:

- 2 1/2 cups all-purpose flour
- 1 cup unsalted butter, chilled and cubed
- 1/2 teaspoon salt
- 1 tablespoon granulated sugar
- 6-8 tablespoons ice water

For the Blueberry Filling:

- 5 cups fresh blueberries, washed and drained
- 1 cup granulated sugar
- 1/4 cup cornstarch
- 1/2 teaspoon ground cinnamon
- 1 tablespoon lemon juice
- Zest of one lemon
- 1 tablespoon butter, cut into small pieces

For Egg Wash:

- 1 egg
- 1 tablespoon water

Instructions:

1. Prepare the Pie Crust:

- In a food processor, combine the flour, salt, and sugar. Add chilled butter cubes and pulse until the mixture resembles coarse crumbs.
- Gradually add ice water, one tablespoon at a time, and pulse until the dough comes together. Be careful not to overmix.
- Divide the dough in half, shape each half into a disk, wrap in plastic wrap, and refrigerate for at least 1 hour.

2. Preheat the Oven:

    - Preheat your oven to 425°F (220°C).

3. Roll Out the Pie Crust:

    - On a floured surface, roll out one of the chilled dough disks to fit a 9-inch pie dish. Place the rolled-out crust into the pie dish.

4. Prepare the Blueberry Filling:

    - In a large bowl, gently toss the blueberries with sugar, cornstarch, cinnamon, lemon juice, and lemon zest until well coated.

5. Assemble the Pie:

    - Pour the blueberry filling into the prepared pie crust. Dot the top with small pieces of butter.
    - Roll out the second dough disk and place it over the blueberry filling. Trim any excess dough and crimp the edges to seal.

6. Make Egg Wash:

    - In a small bowl, whisk together the egg and water to create an egg wash.

7. Bake:

    - Brush the top crust with the egg wash. Cut a few slits on the top crust to allow steam to escape.
    - Place the pie on a baking sheet to catch any drips and bake in the preheated oven for 45-55 minutes or until the crust is golden brown and the filling is bubbly.

8. Cool and Serve:

    - Allow the pie to cool completely on a wire rack before slicing. Serve with a scoop of vanilla ice cream if desired.

This classic blueberry pie is a delightful way to showcase the sweetness of fresh blueberries. Enjoy!

Blueberry Muffins

Ingredients:

- 1 1/2 cups all-purpose flour
- 3/4 cup granulated sugar
- 1/2 teaspoon salt
- 2 teaspoons baking powder
- 1/3 cup vegetable oil
- 1 large egg
- 1/3 cup milk
- 1 teaspoon vanilla extract
- 1 cup fresh or frozen blueberries (if using frozen, do not thaw)

For Streusel Topping:

- 2 tablespoons cold butter, cut into small pieces
- 1/4 cup all-purpose flour
- 2 tablespoons granulated sugar
- 1/2 teaspoon ground cinnamon

Instructions:

1. Preheat the Oven:

- Preheat your oven to 400°F (200°C). Line a muffin tin with paper liners or grease the cups.

2. Make the Streusel Topping:

- In a small bowl, combine the cold butter, flour, sugar, and cinnamon. Use your fingers or a fork to blend the ingredients until crumbly. Set aside.

3. Mix Dry Ingredients:

- In a large bowl, whisk together the flour, sugar, salt, and baking powder.

4. Combine Wet Ingredients:

- In a separate bowl, whisk together the vegetable oil, egg, milk, and vanilla extract.

5. Mix Batter:

- Pour the wet ingredients into the bowl with the dry ingredients. Stir until just combined. Do not overmix; the batter may be a bit lumpy.

6. Add Blueberries:

- Gently fold in the blueberries until evenly distributed in the batter.

7. Fill Muffin Cups:

- Divide the batter evenly among the muffin cups, filling each about 2/3 full.

8. Add Streusel Topping:

- Sprinkle the streusel topping over the muffin batter in each cup.

9. Bake:

- Bake in the preheated oven for 18-20 minutes or until a toothpick inserted into the center comes out clean or with a few moist crumbs.

10. Cool:

- Allow the muffins to cool in the tin for 5 minutes, then transfer them to a wire rack to cool completely.

11. Enjoy:

- Enjoy your homemade blueberry muffins with a cup of coffee or tea!

These blueberry muffins are moist, tender, and bursting with juicy blueberries. They make for a perfect breakfast or snack. Enjoy!

Blueberry Pancakes

Ingredients:

- 1 cup all-purpose flour
- 2 tablespoons granulated sugar
- 1 teaspoon baking powder
- 1/2 teaspoon baking soda
- 1/4 teaspoon salt
- 3/4 cup buttermilk
- 1 large egg
- 2 tablespoons unsalted butter, melted
- 1 teaspoon vanilla extract
- 1 cup fresh blueberries
- Butter or oil for cooking

Instructions:

Prepare Dry Ingredients:
- In a large bowl, whisk together the flour, sugar, baking powder, baking soda, and salt.

Mix Wet Ingredients:
- In another bowl, whisk together the buttermilk, egg, melted butter, and vanilla extract.

Combine Wet and Dry Ingredients:
- Pour the wet ingredients into the dry ingredients and stir until just combined. It's okay if there are a few lumps.

Fold in Blueberries:
- Gently fold in the fresh blueberries. Be careful not to overmix, as this can make the pancakes tough.

Preheat Griddle or Pan:
- Preheat a griddle or non-stick pan over medium heat. Add a small amount of butter or oil to coat the surface.

Spoon Batter onto Griddle:
- Spoon about 1/4 cup of batter onto the griddle for each pancake. Use the back of the spoon to spread the batter into a round shape.

Cook Until Bubbles Form:
- Cook the pancakes until bubbles form on the surface, and the edges start to look set.

Flip and Cook Other Side:
- Carefully flip the pancakes and cook the other side until golden brown.

Serve Warm:
- Once cooked through, transfer the pancakes to a plate and keep warm. Repeat the process with the remaining batter.

Serve and Enjoy:
- Serve the blueberry pancakes warm with your favorite toppings, such as maple syrup, additional blueberries, or a dollop of whipped cream.

These blueberry pancakes are fluffy, flavorful, and a delightful way to start your day!

Blueberry Smoothie

Ingredients:

- 1 cup fresh or frozen blueberries
- 1 banana
- 1/2 cup Greek yogurt
- 1/2 cup milk (dairy or plant-based)
- 1 tablespoon honey or maple syrup (optional, for sweetness)
- 1/2 teaspoon vanilla extract
- Ice cubes (optional)

Instructions:

Combine Ingredients:
- In a blender, add the blueberries, banana, Greek yogurt, milk, honey or maple syrup (if using), and vanilla extract.

Blend Until Smooth:
- Blend the ingredients until smooth and creamy. If the smoothie is too thick, you can add more milk.

Adjust Sweetness:
- Taste the smoothie and add more honey or maple syrup if you prefer a sweeter taste.

Add Ice Cubes (Optional):
- If you like a colder and icier smoothie, you can add a handful of ice cubes and blend again until smooth.

Serve:
- Pour the blueberry smoothie into glasses.

Garnish (Optional):
- Garnish with a few whole blueberries on top for a decorative touch.

Enjoy:
- Refresh yourself with this delicious and nutritious blueberry smoothie!

Feel free to customize the recipe by adding other fruits, greens, or seeds according to your preferences. Enjoy your blueberry smoothie!

Blueberry Cheesecake

Ingredients:

For the Crust:

- 1 1/2 cups graham cracker crumbs
- 1/4 cup melted butter
- 2 tablespoons granulated sugar

For the Cheesecake Filling:

- 4 packages (8 ounces each) cream cheese, softened
- 1 1/4 cups granulated sugar
- 1 teaspoon vanilla extract
- 4 large eggs
- 1/2 cup sour cream
- 1/2 cup all-purpose flour

For the Blueberry Topping:

- 2 cups fresh or frozen blueberries
- 1/2 cup granulated sugar
- 2 tablespoons cornstarch
- 1/4 cup water
- 1 tablespoon lemon juice

Instructions:

1. Preheat the Oven:

- Preheat your oven to 325°F (163°C). Grease a 9-inch springform pan with butter or non-stick cooking spray.

2. Make the Crust:

- In a bowl, combine the graham cracker crumbs, melted butter, and sugar. Press the mixture into the bottom of the prepared springform pan to create an even crust. You can use the back of a spoon to compact it.

3. Prepare the Cheesecake Filling:

    - In a large mixing bowl, beat the cream cheese until smooth using an electric mixer.
    - Add sugar and vanilla extract, and continue to beat until well combined.
    - Add eggs one at a time, beating well after each addition.
    - Mix in sour cream and flour until the batter is smooth and creamy.

4. Pour the Batter:

    - Pour the cheesecake batter over the crust in the springform pan.

5. Bake:

    - Bake in the preheated oven for about 60-70 minutes or until the center is set and the top is golden brown. The edges should be slightly pulling away from the sides of the pan.

6. Cool:

    - Allow the cheesecake to cool in the pan on a wire rack for about 1 hour.

7. Make the Blueberry Topping:

    - In a saucepan, combine blueberries, sugar, cornstarch, water, and lemon juice. Cook over medium heat, stirring frequently until the mixture thickens and the blueberries burst.

8. Chill and Serve:

    - Once the cheesecake has cooled, refrigerate it for at least 4 hours or overnight.
    - Spoon the blueberry topping over the chilled cheesecake just before serving.

9. Enjoy:

- Slice and enjoy your delicious Blueberry Cheesecake!

This classic dessert is sure to be a crowd-pleaser with its creamy texture and flavorful blueberry topping.

Blueberry Jam

Ingredients:

- 4 cups fresh or frozen blueberries
- 1 1/2 cups granulated sugar
- 2 tablespoons lemon juice
- 1 teaspoon lemon zest (optional)
- 1/2 teaspoon butter (optional, to reduce foaming)

Instructions:

Prepare Jars:
- Wash your canning jars, lids, and bands in hot, soapy water. Sterilize them by placing them in a boiling water bath for 10 minutes. Allow them to air dry.

Wash Blueberries:
- If using fresh blueberries, wash them thoroughly. If using frozen blueberries, make sure they are thawed.

Mash Blueberries:
- In a large pot, crush the blueberries using a potato masher or the back of a spoon to release their juices.

Cook Blueberries:
- Add the sugar, lemon juice, and lemon zest (if using) to the crushed blueberries. Stir well to combine.
- Optional: Add a small amount of butter to reduce foaming.

Bring to a Boil:
- Bring the blueberry mixture to a boil over medium-high heat, stirring frequently.

Simmer:
- Reduce the heat to low and let the mixture simmer, stirring occasionally, until it thickens. This can take about 20-30 minutes.

Check for Doneness:
- To check if the jam is ready, place a small amount on a chilled plate. Run your finger through it, and if it wrinkles and holds its shape, it's done.

Skim Foam (Optional):
- If there's foam on the surface, skim it off with a spoon.

Fill Jars:

- Ladle the hot jam into the prepared, sterilized jars, leaving about 1/4-inch headspace.

Seal Jars:
- Wipe the rims of the jars with a clean, damp cloth to remove any residue. Place the sterilized lids on the jars and screw on the bands until fingertip-tight.

Process Jars (Optional):
- If you want to store the jam for an extended period, process the jars in a boiling water bath for about 10 minutes.

Cool and Store:
- Allow the jars to cool to room temperature. Check the lids for a seal by pressing down in the center; if it doesn't pop back, it's sealed.
- Store the sealed jars in a cool, dark place.

Enjoy:
- Once the jam is cooled and set, you can enjoy it on toast, pancakes, or as a topping for various desserts!

Homemade blueberry jam is a delightful treat with the natural sweetness of blueberries. Enjoy spreading it on your favorite baked goods!

Blueberry Scones

Ingredients:

- 2 cups all-purpose flour
- 1/4 cup granulated sugar
- 1 tablespoon baking powder
- 1/2 teaspoon salt
- 1/2 cup unsalted butter, cold and cut into small pieces
- 1 cup fresh or frozen blueberries
- 2/3 cup milk
- 1 teaspoon vanilla extract
- 1 large egg (for egg wash)
- 2 tablespoons coarse sugar (for sprinkling, optional)

Instructions:

Preheat Oven:
- Preheat your oven to 400°F (200°C). Line a baking sheet with parchment paper.

Prepare Dry Ingredients:
- In a large bowl, whisk together the flour, sugar, baking powder, and salt.

Add Butter:
- Add the cold, diced butter to the dry ingredients. Use a pastry cutter or your fingers to work the butter into the flour mixture until it resembles coarse crumbs.

Add Blueberries:
- Gently fold in the blueberries, being careful not to crush them.

Combine Wet Ingredients:
- In a separate bowl, whisk together the milk and vanilla extract.

Mix Dough:
- Pour the wet ingredients into the dry ingredients and stir until just combined. Do not overmix; the dough should be slightly sticky.

Shape Dough:
- Turn the dough out onto a lightly floured surface. Pat it into a circle about 1 inch (2.5 cm) thick.

Cut Scones:
- Use a sharp knife or a round cutter to cut the dough into wedges or rounds.

Egg Wash:
- In a small bowl, beat the egg. Brush the tops of the scones with the egg wash.

Sprinkle Sugar (Optional):
- If desired, sprinkle coarse sugar over the tops of the scones for a sweet crunch.

Bake:
- Place the scones on the prepared baking sheet and bake for 15-18 minutes, or until golden brown.

Cool:
- Allow the scones to cool on the baking sheet for a few minutes, then transfer them to a wire rack to cool completely.

Serve:
- Serve the blueberry scones with clotted cream, jam, or enjoy them on their own.

These blueberry scones are a delightful addition to breakfast or tea time. The burst of blueberries and the flaky, buttery texture make them a perfect treat!

Blueberry Cobbler

Ingredients:

For the Filling:

- 4 cups fresh or frozen blueberries
- 1/2 cup granulated sugar
- 1 tablespoon lemon juice
- 1 tablespoon cornstarch

For the Cobbler Topping:

- 1 cup all-purpose flour
- 1/2 cup granulated sugar
- 1 teaspoon baking powder
- 1/4 teaspoon salt
- 1/2 cup unsalted butter, cold and cut into small pieces
- 1/4 cup boiling water

Instructions:

Preheat Oven:
- Preheat your oven to 375°F (190°C).

Prepare Filling:
- In a large bowl, gently toss together the blueberries, sugar, lemon juice, and cornstarch until well combined. Transfer the blueberry mixture to a baking dish (8x8 inches or a similar size).

Make Cobbler Topping:
- In a separate bowl, combine the flour, sugar, baking powder, and salt for the cobbler topping. Cut in the cold butter using a pastry cutter or your fingers until the mixture resembles coarse crumbs.

Add Boiling Water:
- Pour the boiling water over the flour-butter mixture and stir until just combined. The batter will be thick.

Drop Batter onto Blueberries:
- Drop spoonfuls of the cobbler batter onto the blueberry filling. It's okay if it doesn't completely cover the surface.

Bake:

- Bake in the preheated oven for about 40-45 minutes or until the cobbler topping is golden brown and the blueberry filling is bubbling.

Cool:
- Allow the blueberry cobbler to cool for a few minutes before serving.

Serve:
- Serve warm, optionally with a scoop of vanilla ice cream or a dollop of whipped cream.

Enjoy the comforting and delicious taste of homemade blueberry cobbler! The sweet and juicy blueberry filling combined with the buttery cobbler topping makes for a delightful treat.

Blueberry Lemonade

Ingredients:

- 1 cup fresh or frozen blueberries
- 1 cup granulated sugar
- 1 cup freshly squeezed lemon juice (about 4-6 lemons)
- 4 cups cold water
- Ice cubes
- Fresh mint leaves for garnish (optional)
- Lemon slices for garnish (optional)

Instructions:

Make Blueberry Syrup:
- In a small saucepan, combine the blueberries and sugar. Heat over medium heat, stirring occasionally, until the blueberries burst and the sugar dissolves, creating a syrup. This usually takes about 5-7 minutes.

Strain Blueberry Syrup:
- Strain the blueberry mixture through a fine-mesh sieve into a bowl, pressing down to extract as much liquid as possible. Discard the solids.

Prepare Lemonade Base:
- In a large pitcher, combine the freshly squeezed lemon juice and cold water. Stir well.

Add Blueberry Syrup:
- Pour the strained blueberry syrup into the pitcher with the lemonade base. Stir until well combined. Adjust the sweetness by adding more sugar if needed, based on your preference.

Chill:
- Refrigerate the blueberry lemonade for at least 1-2 hours to allow the flavors to meld and the drink to chill.

Serve:
- Fill glasses with ice cubes and pour the blueberry lemonade over the ice.

Garnish (Optional):
- Garnish the blueberry lemonade with fresh mint leaves and lemon slices for a decorative touch.

Enjoy:
- Stir before serving, and enjoy the refreshing and fruity flavor of homemade Blueberry Lemonade!

This blueberry-infused lemonade is perfect for hot summer days or any time you crave a vibrant and flavorful beverage.

Blueberry Ice Cream

Ingredients:

- 2 cups fresh or frozen blueberries
- 1 cup granulated sugar
- 1 tablespoon lemon juice
- 2 cups heavy cream
- 1 cup whole milk
- 1 teaspoon vanilla extract

Instructions:

Blueberry Sauce:
- In a medium saucepan, combine the blueberries, sugar, and lemon juice. Cook over medium heat, stirring occasionally, until the blueberries burst and the mixture thickens into a sauce. This usually takes about 10-15 minutes. Remove from heat and let it cool.

Blend Blueberry Sauce:
- Once the blueberry sauce has cooled, blend it in a blender or use an immersion blender until smooth. Set aside.

Ice Cream Base:
- In a mixing bowl, whisk together the heavy cream, whole milk, and vanilla extract until well combined.

Combine Blueberry Sauce and Ice Cream Base:
- Pour the blueberry sauce into the ice cream base and stir until evenly mixed.

Chill:
- Cover the bowl and refrigerate the mixture for at least 2 hours or overnight to chill thoroughly.

Churn:
- Pour the chilled blueberry ice cream mixture into an ice cream maker and churn according to the manufacturer's instructions until it reaches a soft-serve consistency.

Freeze:
- Transfer the churned ice cream to a lidded container. Swirl in additional blueberry sauce if desired. Cover and freeze for at least 4 hours or until firm.

Serve and Enjoy:

- Scoop the blueberry ice cream into bowls or cones and enjoy the homemade goodness!

This blueberry ice cream is a delightful treat with the sweet and tangy flavor of blueberries combined with the creamy richness of the ice cream base. Perfect for a summer day or any time you're craving a cool and fruity dessert!

Blueberry Crisp

Ingredients:

For the Blueberry Filling:

- 4 cups fresh or frozen blueberries
- 1/2 cup granulated sugar
- 2 tablespoons cornstarch
- 1 tablespoon lemon juice
- 1 teaspoon vanilla extract

For the Crisp Topping:

- 1 cup old-fashioned oats
- 1/2 cup all-purpose flour
- 1/2 cup packed brown sugar
- 1/4 teaspoon salt
- 1/2 cup unsalted butter, cold and diced

Instructions:

Preheat Oven:
- Preheat your oven to 350°F (175°C). Grease a baking dish (8x8 inches or a similar size).

Prepare Blueberry Filling:
- In a large bowl, combine the blueberries, granulated sugar, cornstarch, lemon juice, and vanilla extract. Toss until the blueberries are well coated. Transfer the blueberry mixture to the prepared baking dish.

Make Crisp Topping:
- In a separate bowl, mix together the oats, flour, brown sugar, and salt. Add the cold diced butter. Use your fingers or a pastry cutter to incorporate the butter into the dry ingredients until the mixture resembles coarse crumbs.

Top Blueberries with Crisp Mixture:
- Sprinkle the crisp topping evenly over the blueberry mixture in the baking dish.

Bake:
- Bake in the preheated oven for about 40-45 minutes or until the blueberry filling is bubbly, and the crisp topping is golden brown.

Cool and Serve:
- Allow the blueberry crisp to cool for a few minutes before serving. Serve it warm with a scoop of vanilla ice cream or a dollop of whipped cream if desired.

Enjoy:
- Enjoy this delightful blueberry crisp as a comforting dessert.

This blueberry crisp is a perfect way to showcase the sweet and juicy flavor of fresh blueberries. The combination of the fruity filling and the crunchy oat topping makes for a delicious and satisfying dessert.

Blueberry Banana Bread

Ingredients:

- 3 ripe bananas, mashed
- 1/2 cup unsalted butter, melted
- 1 teaspoon vanilla extract
- 1/2 cup granulated sugar
- 1/2 cup brown sugar, packed
- 2 large eggs
- 2 cups all-purpose flour
- 1 teaspoon baking soda
- 1/2 teaspoon baking powder
- 1/2 teaspoon salt
- 1 cup fresh or frozen blueberries (if using frozen, do not thaw)
- Optional: 1/2 cup chopped nuts (walnuts or pecans)

Instructions:

Preheat Oven:
- Preheat your oven to 350°F (175°C). Grease a 9x5-inch loaf pan.

Mash Bananas:
- In a large mixing bowl, mash the ripe bananas with a fork or potato masher.

Mix Wet Ingredients:
- Add melted butter, vanilla extract, granulated sugar, brown sugar, and eggs to the mashed bananas. Mix well until the ingredients are combined.

Combine Dry Ingredients:
- In a separate bowl, whisk together the flour, baking soda, baking powder, and salt.

Combine Wet and Dry Ingredients:
- Gradually add the dry ingredients to the wet ingredients, mixing just until combined. Be careful not to overmix.

Fold in Blueberries (and Nuts):
- Gently fold in the blueberries (and chopped nuts if using).

Transfer to Loaf Pan:
- Pour the batter into the prepared loaf pan, spreading it evenly.

Bake:

- Bake in the preheated oven for about 60-70 minutes or until a toothpick inserted into the center comes out clean or with a few moist crumbs (avoiding blueberry stains).

Cool:
- Allow the banana bread to cool in the pan for about 10 minutes, then transfer it to a wire rack to cool completely.

Slice and Enjoy:
- Once cooled, slice the blueberry banana bread into slices and enjoy!

This Blueberry Banana Bread is a wonderful combination of moist banana bread with bursts of juicy blueberries. It's perfect for breakfast, brunch, or as a sweet treat any time of the day!

Blueberry Oatmeal Bars

Ingredients:

For the Crust and Topping:

- 1 1/2 cups old-fashioned oats
- 1 1/2 cups all-purpose flour
- 1 cup light brown sugar, packed
- 1/2 teaspoon baking powder
- 1/4 teaspoon salt
- 1 cup unsalted butter, melted

For the Blueberry Filling:

- 3 cups fresh or frozen blueberries
- 1/2 cup granulated sugar
- 2 tablespoons lemon juice
- 2 tablespoons cornstarch

Instructions:

Preheat Oven:
- Preheat your oven to 350°F (175°C). Grease a 9x13-inch baking dish.

Make the Crust and Topping:
- In a large mixing bowl, combine the oats, flour, brown sugar, baking powder, and salt. Add the melted butter and mix until the mixture resembles coarse crumbs.

Reserve Some Mixture:
- Take about 1 1/2 cups of the mixture and set it aside to use as the topping.

Press Crust:
- Press the remaining mixture into the bottom of the prepared baking dish to form an even crust.

Make the Blueberry Filling:
- In another bowl, combine the blueberries, sugar, lemon juice, and cornstarch. Toss until the blueberries are well coated.

Layer the Blueberry Filling:
- Spread the blueberry mixture evenly over the crust in the baking dish.

Add Topping:
- Sprinkle the reserved oat mixture evenly over the blueberry filling.

Bake:
- Bake in the preheated oven for 40-45 minutes or until the topping is golden brown and the blueberry filling is bubbly.

Cool:
- Allow the bars to cool completely in the baking dish on a wire rack.

Cut and Serve:
- Once cooled, cut into squares or bars. Serve and enjoy!

These Blueberry Oatmeal Bars are a delightful combination of a buttery oat crust, sweet blueberry filling, and a crumbly topping. They make for a perfect snack or dessert, and they're great for gatherings or as a sweet treat for your family.

Blueberry Parfait

Ingredients:

- 2 cups fresh blueberries
- 2 cups Greek yogurt
- 1/4 cup honey or maple syrup
- 1 teaspoon vanilla extract
- 1 cup granola

Instructions:

Prepare Blueberries:
- Wash the blueberries and set aside.

Prepare Greek Yogurt:
- In a bowl, mix Greek yogurt with honey or maple syrup and vanilla extract. Adjust sweetness according to your preference.

Layering:
- In serving glasses or bowls, start by adding a layer of the Greek yogurt mixture at the bottom.
- Add a layer of fresh blueberries on top of the yogurt.
- Sprinkle a layer of granola over the blueberries.

Repeat Layers:
- Repeat the layers until you reach the top of the glass or bowl, finishing with a layer of blueberries and a sprinkle of granola.

Serve:
- Serve immediately and enjoy!

This Blueberry Parfait is not only visually appealing with its layers but also offers a delightful combination of creamy yogurt, sweet blueberries, and crunchy granola. It's a healthy and satisfying treat that can be enjoyed for breakfast, as a snack, or as a light dessert. Feel free to customize it with additional toppings like nuts or shredded coconut if desired.

Blueberry Breakfast Casserole

Ingredients:

- 1 loaf of French bread, cut into cubes
- 2 cups fresh or frozen blueberries
- 8 large eggs
- 2 cups milk (whole milk or any milk of your choice)
- 1/2 cup maple syrup
- 1 teaspoon vanilla extract
- 1 teaspoon ground cinnamon
- 1/2 teaspoon salt
- 1/2 cup unsalted butter, melted
- Maple syrup or powdered sugar for serving (optional)

Instructions:

Preheat your oven to 350°F (175°C). Grease a 9x13 inch baking dish.
Place half of the bread cubes in the prepared baking dish, and sprinkle half of the blueberries over the bread.
Add the remaining bread cubes on top, followed by the remaining blueberries.
In a large mixing bowl, whisk together the eggs, milk, maple syrup, vanilla extract, ground cinnamon, and salt.
Pour the egg mixture evenly over the bread and blueberries. Gently press down on the bread with a spatula to ensure all the bread cubes are soaked in the egg mixture.
Drizzle the melted butter over the top.
Let the casserole sit for about 10-15 minutes to allow the bread to absorb the liquid.
Bake in the preheated oven for 45-50 minutes or until the top is golden brown and the center is set.
Remove from the oven and let it cool for a few minutes before serving.
Optional: Drizzle with additional maple syrup or dust with powdered sugar before serving.

This blueberry breakfast casserole is a delightful blend of sweet and comforting flavors, making it a perfect dish for a weekend brunch or special occasions. Enjoy!

Blueberry Vinaigrette Salad

Ingredients:

- 1 cup fresh or frozen blueberries
- 1/4 cup balsamic vinegar
- 1/3 cup olive oil
- 1 tablespoon honey or maple syrup
- 1 teaspoon Dijon mustard
- Salt and pepper to taste

Salad:

Feel free to customize your salad with a mix of your favorite greens and toppings. Here's a suggested combination:

- Mixed salad greens (spinach, arugula, or lettuce)
- Cherry tomatoes, halved
- Cucumber, sliced
- Red onion, thinly sliced
- Feta cheese or goat cheese, crumbled
- Candied nuts or toasted almonds

Instructions:

Prepare the Blueberry Vinaigrette:
- In a blender or food processor, combine the blueberries, balsamic vinegar, olive oil, honey (or maple syrup), Dijon mustard, salt, and pepper.
- Blend until smooth and well combined. If the vinaigrette is too thick, you can add a bit more olive oil to reach your desired consistency.

Assemble the Salad:
- In a large salad bowl, toss together the mixed salad greens, cherry tomatoes, cucumber, and red onion.

Serve:
- Drizzle the blueberry vinaigrette over the salad just before serving. Toss the salad gently to coat the ingredients evenly.

Add Toppings:

- Sprinkle crumbled feta cheese or goat cheese on top of the salad.
- Optionally, add candied nuts or toasted almonds for a crunchy texture.

Enjoy:
- Serve the blueberry vinaigrette salad immediately as a refreshing and flavorful side dish or a light meal.

This blueberry vinaigrette salad is not only delicious but also packed with antioxidants and nutrients. It's a perfect option for a summer salad or whenever you want a burst of fruity goodness in your greens.

Blueberry Cheesecake Bars

Ingredients:

For the Crust:

- 1 1/2 cups graham cracker crumbs
- 1/3 cup melted butter
- 2 tablespoons granulated sugar

For the Cheesecake Filling:

- 16 ounces (2 packages) cream cheese, softened
- 2/3 cup granulated sugar
- 2 large eggs
- 1 teaspoon vanilla extract
- 1/4 cup all-purpose flour

For the Blueberry Topping:

- 1 1/2 cups fresh or frozen blueberries
- 1/4 cup granulated sugar
- 1 tablespoon lemon juice
- 1 teaspoon cornstarch

Instructions:

Preheat the Oven:
- Preheat your oven to 325°F (163°C). Grease or line a 9x9-inch baking pan with parchment paper, leaving some overhang for easy removal.

Prepare the Crust:
- In a medium bowl, combine graham cracker crumbs, melted butter, and sugar. Press the mixture firmly into the bottom of the prepared baking pan to form an even crust.

Prepare the Cheesecake Filling:
- In a large mixing bowl, beat the softened cream cheese until smooth.

- Add sugar, eggs, vanilla extract, and flour. Beat until well combined and smooth.

Pour and Smooth:
- Pour the cream cheese mixture over the crust in the baking pan. Use a spatula to smooth the top evenly.

Prepare the Blueberry Topping:
- In a saucepan, combine blueberries, sugar, lemon juice, and cornstarch. Cook over medium heat, stirring continuously until the mixture thickens and the blueberries burst slightly.

Add Blueberry Topping:
- Spoon the blueberry mixture over the cream cheese layer, spreading it evenly.

Bake:
- Bake in the preheated oven for about 40-45 minutes or until the edges are set, and the center is slightly jiggly.

Cool and Chill:
- Allow the bars to cool completely at room temperature, then refrigerate for at least 3 hours or overnight for the best texture.

Slice and Serve:
- Once chilled, use the parchment paper overhang to lift the cheesecake out of the pan. Cut into squares, and serve.

Enjoy these Blueberry Cheesecake Bars as a delightful treat for dessert, parties, or any special occasion!

Blueberry and Almond Granola

Ingredients:

- 3 cups old-fashioned rolled oats
- 1 cup sliced almonds
- 1/2 cup shredded coconut (optional)
- 1/3 cup honey or maple syrup
- 1/4 cup coconut oil, melted
- 1 teaspoon vanilla extract
- 1/2 teaspoon almond extract (optional)
- 1/2 teaspoon ground cinnamon
- 1/4 teaspoon salt
- 1 cup dried blueberries

Instructions:

Preheat the Oven:
- Preheat your oven to 325°F (163°C). Line a large baking sheet with parchment paper.

Mix Dry Ingredients:
- In a large bowl, combine the rolled oats, sliced almonds, and shredded coconut (if using).

Prepare the Wet Ingredients:
- In a separate bowl, whisk together the honey or maple syrup, melted coconut oil, vanilla extract, almond extract (if using), ground cinnamon, and salt.

Combine Wet and Dry Ingredients:
- Pour the wet ingredients over the dry ingredients and mix well until the oats and nuts are evenly coated.

Spread on Baking Sheet:
- Spread the granola mixture evenly on the prepared baking sheet in a single layer.

Bake:
- Bake in the preheated oven for about 25-30 minutes, stirring halfway through, or until the granola is golden brown.

Add Blueberries:
- Remove the baking sheet from the oven and stir in the dried blueberries.

Cool:

- Allow the granola to cool completely on the baking sheet. It will continue to crisp up as it cools.

Store:
- Once completely cooled, transfer the blueberry and almond granola to an airtight container for storage.

Serve:
- Enjoy the granola with yogurt, milk, or as a topping for smoothie bowls.

Feel free to customize this recipe by adding other ingredients such as chia seeds, flaxseeds, or your favorite nuts and seeds. Homemade granola is not only delicious but also allows you to control the sweetness and tailor it to your taste preferences.

Blueberry Glazed Salmon

Ingredients:

For the Blueberry Glaze:

- 1 cup fresh or frozen blueberries
- 1/4 cup balsamic vinegar
- 2 tablespoons honey or maple syrup
- 1 teaspoon Dijon mustard
- Salt and pepper to taste

For the Salmon:

- 4 salmon fillets
- Salt and pepper to taste
- 1 tablespoon olive oil
- Fresh lemon wedges for serving (optional)

Instructions:

Prepare the Blueberry Glaze:
- In a saucepan, combine the blueberries, balsamic vinegar, honey (or maple syrup), Dijon mustard, salt, and pepper.
- Bring the mixture to a simmer over medium heat. Cook for about 8-10 minutes, or until the blueberries burst and the sauce thickens. Stir occasionally to prevent sticking.

Blend the Glaze (Optional):
- For a smoother glaze, you can use an immersion blender or transfer the mixture to a blender to puree until smooth. Strain if desired for a smoother consistency.

Prepare the Salmon:
- Preheat your oven to 400°F (200°C).
- Season the salmon fillets with salt and pepper.

Sear the Salmon:
- In an oven-safe skillet, heat olive oil over medium-high heat.
- Sear the salmon fillets, skin-side down, for 2-3 minutes until the skin is crispy.

Apply Blueberry Glaze:

- Spoon a generous amount of the blueberry glaze over the salmon fillets, ensuring they are well-coated.

Bake:
- Transfer the skillet to the preheated oven and bake for 10-12 minutes or until the salmon is cooked through and flakes easily with a fork.

Broil (Optional):
- If you want a caramelized finish, you can broil the salmon for an additional 1-2 minutes, keeping a close eye to prevent burning.

Serve:
- Serve the blueberry glazed salmon hot, drizzled with additional blueberry glaze if desired.
- Garnish with fresh lemon wedges for a burst of citrus flavor.

This Blueberry Glazed Salmon is a delightful combination of sweet and savory, making it a perfect choice for a special dinner. Enjoy!

Blueberry Greek Yogurt Popsicles

Ingredients:

- 1 cup fresh or frozen blueberries
- 2 tablespoons honey or maple syrup (adjust to taste)
- 1 tablespoon lemon juice
- 1 1/2 cups Greek yogurt (plain or vanilla flavored)
- 1/2 cup milk (dairy or plant-based)
- 1 teaspoon vanilla extract (if using plain Greek yogurt)
- Popsicle molds

Instructions:

Prepare the Blueberry Puree:
- In a blender or food processor, combine the blueberries, honey or maple syrup, and lemon juice.
- Blend until you have a smooth blueberry puree. If the mixture is too thick, you can add a splash of water to help with blending.

Prepare the Yogurt Mixture:
- In a separate bowl, mix together the Greek yogurt, milk, and vanilla extract (if using plain Greek yogurt). Stir until well combined.

Layer the Popsicles:
- Begin by spooning a layer of the blueberry puree into each popsicle mold, filling it about one-third of the way.
- Follow with a layer of the Greek yogurt mixture, filling another one-third of the mold.
- Repeat the layers until the molds are nearly full, finishing with a layer of blueberry puree on top.

Swirl or Layer Effect (Optional):
- Use a popsicle stick or a skewer to gently swirl the layers together for a marbled effect.

Insert Popsicle Sticks:
- Insert popsicle sticks into the center of each mold.

Freeze:
- Place the popsicle molds in the freezer and let them freeze for at least 4-6 hours, or until completely set.

Unmold and Enjoy:

- Once the popsicles are fully frozen, remove them from the molds by running them under warm water for a few seconds. This helps release the popsicles easily.

Serve:
- Enjoy these Blueberry Greek Yogurt Popsicles on a hot day as a healthy and refreshing snack.

Feel free to customize this recipe by adding other fruits, such as strawberries or raspberries, for a mixed berry version. These popsicles are a great way to enjoy the goodness of Greek yogurt and the natural sweetness of blueberries.

Blueberry Almond Cake

Ingredients:

For the Cake:

- 1 cup all-purpose flour
- 1 cup almond flour
- 1 teaspoon baking powder
- 1/2 teaspoon baking soda
- 1/4 teaspoon salt
- 1/2 cup unsalted butter, softened
- 3/4 cup granulated sugar
- 2 large eggs
- 1 teaspoon almond extract
- 1/2 cup plain Greek yogurt
- 1 cup fresh or frozen blueberries

For the Almond Streusel Topping:

- 1/2 cup sliced almonds
- 2 tablespoons granulated sugar
- 1 tablespoon all-purpose flour
- 2 tablespoons unsalted butter, melted

Instructions:

Preheat the Oven:
- Preheat your oven to 350°F (175°C). Grease and flour a 9-inch round cake pan.

Prepare the Almond Streusel Topping:
- In a small bowl, mix together the sliced almonds, sugar, flour, and melted butter until it forms a crumbly texture. Set aside.

Make the Cake Batter:
- In a medium bowl, whisk together the all-purpose flour, almond flour, baking powder, baking soda, and salt.
- In a separate large bowl, cream together the softened butter and granulated sugar until light and fluffy. Add the eggs one at a time, beating well after each addition. Stir in the almond extract.

- Gradually add the dry ingredients to the wet ingredients, alternating with the Greek yogurt, beginning and ending with the dry ingredients. Mix until just combined.

Fold in Blueberries:
- Gently fold in the blueberries until evenly distributed throughout the batter.

Assemble and Bake:
- Pour the cake batter into the prepared cake pan, spreading it evenly.
- Sprinkle the almond streusel topping over the batter, covering it evenly.
- Bake in the preheated oven for approximately 40-45 minutes, or until a toothpick inserted into the center comes out clean.

Cool:
- Allow the cake to cool in the pan for 10 minutes, then transfer it to a wire rack to cool completely.

Serve:
- Once cooled, slice and serve the Blueberry Almond Cake. Optionally, dust with powdered sugar before serving.

This cake is a wonderful combination of moist almond cake and bursts of sweetness from the blueberries. It's perfect for tea time, dessert, or any special occasion. Enjoy!

Blueberry BBQ Sauce

Ingredients:

- 2 cups fresh or frozen blueberries
- 1 cup ketchup
- 1/2 cup apple cider vinegar
- 1/4 cup brown sugar
- 2 tablespoons honey or maple syrup
- 1 tablespoon Worcestershire sauce
- 1 teaspoon Dijon mustard
- 1 teaspoon smoked paprika
- 1/2 teaspoon garlic powder
- 1/2 teaspoon onion powder
- Salt and black pepper to taste

Instructions:

Prepare the Blueberry Base:
- In a medium saucepan, combine the blueberries, ketchup, apple cider vinegar, brown sugar, and honey or maple syrup.

Add Flavorings:
- Stir in Worcestershire sauce, Dijon mustard, smoked paprika, garlic powder, onion powder, salt, and black pepper.

Simmer:
- Place the saucepan over medium heat and bring the mixture to a simmer. Once simmering, reduce the heat to low and let it cook for about 15-20 minutes, stirring occasionally.

Mash Blueberries (Optional):
- If you prefer a smoother sauce, you can use a potato masher or an immersion blender to break down the blueberries and achieve a smoother consistency.

Adjust Seasoning:
- Taste the sauce and adjust the sweetness, acidity, or seasoning according to your preferences. Add more honey, vinegar, or salt if needed.

Cool and Store:
- Allow the Blueberry BBQ Sauce to cool before transferring it to a jar or airtight container. Refrigerate until ready to use.

Use as a Glaze or Sauce:

- Brush the Blueberry BBQ Sauce onto grilled chicken, pork, or beef during the last few minutes of cooking, or use it as a dipping sauce.

This Blueberry BBQ Sauce brings a sweet and tangy flavor with a hint of smokiness, making it a delightful addition to your barbecue repertoire. Experiment with it on various meats or use it as a flavorful condiment for burgers and sandwiches.

Blueberry Shortcake

Ingredients:

For the Shortcakes:

- 2 cups all-purpose flour
- 1/4 cup granulated sugar
- 1 tablespoon baking powder
- 1/2 teaspoon salt
- 1/2 cup unsalted butter, cold and cut into small pieces
- 2/3 cup milk
- 1 teaspoon vanilla extract

For the Blueberry Filling:

- 4 cups fresh blueberries
- 1/2 cup granulated sugar
- 1 tablespoon lemon juice
- Zest of one lemon

For the Whipped Cream:

- 1 cup heavy cream
- 2 tablespoons powdered sugar
- 1 teaspoon vanilla extract

Instructions:

Preheat the Oven:
- Preheat your oven to 425°F (220°C). Line a baking sheet with parchment paper.

Prepare the Shortcakes:
- In a large mixing bowl, whisk together the flour, sugar, baking powder, and salt.

- Add the cold, diced butter to the flour mixture. Use a pastry cutter or your fingers to cut the butter into the flour until the mixture resembles coarse crumbs.
- Pour in the milk and vanilla extract. Stir until just combined, being careful not to overmix.
- Turn the dough out onto a floured surface. Pat it into a rectangle about 1 inch thick. Use a round biscuit cutter to cut out shortcakes.
- Place the shortcakes on the prepared baking sheet and bake for 12-15 minutes, or until they are golden brown.

Prepare the Blueberry Filling:
- In a bowl, combine the fresh blueberries, granulated sugar, lemon juice, and lemon zest. Gently toss to coat the blueberries evenly in the sugar mixture. Allow it to sit and macerate for about 15 minutes.

Prepare the Whipped Cream:
- In a separate bowl, whip the heavy cream, powdered sugar, and vanilla extract until stiff peaks form.

Assemble the Blueberry Shortcakes:
- Once the shortcakes have cooled, slice them in half horizontally.
- Spoon a generous amount of the macerated blueberries onto the bottom half of each shortcake.
- Add a dollop of whipped cream on top of the blueberries.
- Place the top half of the shortcake over the whipped cream to form a sandwich.

Serve:
- Serve the Blueberry Shortcakes immediately. Optionally, you can drizzle some of the macerated blueberry juice over the top for extra flavor.

This Blueberry Shortcake is a delightful summertime dessert, showcasing the natural sweetness of blueberries and the richness of whipped cream nestled between tender, homemade shortcakes. Enjoy!

Blueberry and Goat Cheese Salad

Ingredients:

For the Salad:

- 6 cups mixed salad greens (e.g., arugula, spinach, or spring mix)
- 1 cup fresh blueberries
- 1/2 cup candied pecans or walnuts, roughly chopped
- 4 ounces goat cheese, crumbled
- 1/4 cup red onion, thinly sliced

For the Vinaigrette:

- 1/4 cup extra-virgin olive oil
- 2 tablespoons balsamic vinegar
- 1 tablespoon honey
- Salt and pepper to taste

Instructions:

Prepare the Salad Greens:
- In a large salad bowl, combine the mixed salad greens.

Add Blueberries and Goat Cheese:
- Sprinkle the fresh blueberries, crumbled goat cheese, candied pecans or walnuts, and thinly sliced red onion over the salad greens.

Make the Vinaigrette:
- In a small bowl or jar, whisk together the extra-virgin olive oil, balsamic vinegar, honey, salt, and pepper. Adjust the sweetness and acidity to your liking.

Dress the Salad:
- Drizzle the vinaigrette over the salad just before serving. Toss the salad gently to coat the ingredients evenly with the dressing.

Serve:
- Transfer the salad to individual serving plates or bowls.

Optional Additions:
- For added protein, you can include grilled chicken or shrimp on top.

- Avocado slices can also be a tasty addition for extra creaminess.

Enjoy:
- Serve the Blueberry and Goat Cheese Salad immediately, enjoying the vibrant flavors and textures.

This salad is a perfect combination of sweet, savory, and tangy elements, making it a wonderful choice for a light lunch or a side dish for dinner. The blueberries add a burst of freshness, while the goat cheese provides a creamy and tangy balance.

Blueberry Lemon Loaf

Ingredients:

For the Loaf:

- 1/2 cup unsalted butter, softened
- 1 cup granulated sugar
- 2 large eggs
- 1 teaspoon vanilla extract
- 1 tablespoon lemon zest (from about 2 lemons)
- 1 1/2 cups all-purpose flour
- 1 1/2 teaspoons baking powder
- 1/4 teaspoon baking soda
- 1/4 teaspoon salt
- 1/2 cup sour cream or Greek yogurt
- 1 1/2 cups fresh blueberries (tossed in 1 tablespoon of flour to prevent sinking)

For the Lemon Glaze:

- 1 cup powdered sugar
- 2 tablespoons fresh lemon juice

Instructions:

Preheat the Oven:
- Preheat your oven to 350°F (175°C). Grease and flour a 9x5-inch loaf pan.

Cream Butter and Sugar:
- In a large bowl, cream together the softened butter and granulated sugar until light and fluffy.

Add Eggs and Vanilla:
- Add the eggs one at a time, beating well after each addition. Stir in the vanilla extract and lemon zest.

Combine Dry Ingredients:
- In a separate bowl, whisk together the flour, baking powder, baking soda, and salt.

Add Dry Ingredients to Wet Ingredients:
- Gradually add the dry ingredients to the wet ingredients, mixing just until combined.

Add Sour Cream:
- Fold in the sour cream or Greek yogurt until smooth.

Fold in Blueberries:
- Gently fold the blueberries (coated in flour) into the batter.

Bake:
- Pour the batter into the prepared loaf pan and smooth the top. Bake in the preheated oven for about 50-60 minutes, or until a toothpick inserted into the center comes out clean.

Cool:
- Allow the Blueberry Lemon Loaf to cool in the pan for 15 minutes, then transfer it to a wire rack to cool completely.

Prepare Lemon Glaze:
- In a small bowl, whisk together the powdered sugar and fresh lemon juice until smooth.

Drizzle Glaze:
- Once the loaf is completely cooled, drizzle the lemon glaze over the top.

Slice and Serve:
- Slice and serve the Blueberry Lemon Loaf, enjoying the burst of citrus and sweetness.

This Blueberry Lemon Loaf is perfect for breakfast, brunch, or as a delightful dessert. The combination of lemon and blueberries creates a vibrant and delicious treat that's sure to be a hit.

Blueberry Balsamic Chicken

Ingredients:

- 4 boneless, skinless chicken breasts
- Salt and black pepper to taste
- 1 tablespoon olive oil
- 1/2 cup balsamic vinegar
- 1 cup fresh or frozen blueberries
- 2 tablespoons honey or maple syrup
- 2 cloves garlic, minced
- 1 teaspoon dried thyme (or 1 tablespoon fresh thyme)
- 1/2 cup chicken broth
- Fresh basil or parsley for garnish (optional)

Instructions:

Season Chicken:
- Season the chicken breasts with salt and black pepper to taste.

Sear Chicken:
- In a large skillet, heat olive oil over medium-high heat. Add the chicken breasts and sear for 2-3 minutes on each side until browned. Remove the chicken from the skillet and set aside.

Prepare Blueberry Balsamic Sauce:
- In the same skillet, add balsamic vinegar, blueberries, honey or maple syrup, minced garlic, and dried thyme. Stir to combine.

Simmer:
- Reduce the heat to medium and let the mixture simmer for 5-7 minutes, allowing the blueberries to break down and the sauce to thicken.

Add Chicken Broth:
- Pour in the chicken broth and stir to combine. Allow the sauce to simmer for an additional 2-3 minutes.

Return Chicken to Skillet:
- Return the seared chicken breasts to the skillet, spooning some of the blueberry balsamic sauce over them.

Finish Cooking:
- Continue cooking the chicken in the sauce for about 8-10 minutes, or until the chicken is cooked through. The internal temperature should reach 165°F (74°C).

Garnish and Serve:
- Garnish with fresh basil or parsley if desired. Serve the Blueberry Balsamic Chicken hot.

Optional: Reduce Sauce (Optional):
- If you desire a thicker sauce, you can remove the chicken from the skillet once it's cooked and continue simmering the sauce until it reaches your desired consistency.

Serve:
- Serve the Blueberry Balsamic Chicken over rice, quinoa, or with your favorite side dishes.

This dish offers a delightful combination of savory and sweet flavors, making it a unique and delicious option for a special dinner. Enjoy!

Blueberry Spinach Salad

Ingredients:

For the Salad:

- 6 cups fresh baby spinach leaves, washed and dried
- 1 cup fresh blueberries
- 1/2 cup crumbled feta cheese
- 1/2 cup sliced almonds, toasted
- 1/4 cup red onion, thinly sliced

For the Lemon Poppy Seed Dressing:

- 1/4 cup olive oil
- 2 tablespoons fresh lemon juice
- 1 tablespoon honey
- 1 teaspoon Dijon mustard
- 1 teaspoon poppy seeds
- Salt and pepper to taste

Instructions:

Prepare the Salad:
- In a large salad bowl, combine the baby spinach, blueberries, crumbled feta cheese, toasted sliced almonds, and thinly sliced red onion.

Make the Lemon Poppy Seed Dressing:
- In a small bowl or jar, whisk together the olive oil, fresh lemon juice, honey, Dijon mustard, poppy seeds, salt, and pepper. Adjust the sweetness and acidity to your liking.

Dress the Salad:
- Drizzle the lemon poppy seed dressing over the salad just before serving. Toss the salad gently to coat the ingredients evenly with the dressing.

Serve:
- Transfer the Blueberry Spinach Salad to individual serving plates or bowls.

Optional Additions:
- For extra protein, you can add grilled chicken or shrimp on top of the salad.
- Avocado slices can also be a tasty addition for creaminess.

Enjoy:
- Serve the Blueberry Spinach Salad immediately, savoring the combination of sweet blueberries, crunchy almonds, and tangy feta with the freshness of spinach.

This salad is not only delicious but also packed with antioxidants and nutrients. It's a perfect choice for a light and healthy lunch or as a side dish for dinner.

Blueberry and Ricotta Pancakes

Ingredients:

- 1 cup all-purpose flour
- 2 tablespoons granulated sugar
- 1 teaspoon baking powder
- 1/2 teaspoon baking soda
- 1/4 teaspoon salt
- 1 cup ricotta cheese
- 3/4 cup milk
- 2 large eggs
- 1 teaspoon vanilla extract
- 1 cup fresh or frozen blueberries
- Butter or cooking spray for greasing the pan

Instructions:

Prepare Dry Ingredients:
- In a large bowl, whisk together the flour, sugar, baking powder, baking soda, and salt.

Combine Wet Ingredients:
- In another bowl, whisk together the ricotta cheese, milk, eggs, and vanilla extract until well combined.

Combine Wet and Dry Ingredients:
- Pour the wet ingredients into the dry ingredients and stir until just combined. Do not overmix; it's okay if there are a few lumps.

Add Blueberries:
- Gently fold in the blueberries into the pancake batter.

Preheat the Griddle or Pan:
- Preheat a griddle or non-stick pan over medium heat. Add a small amount of butter or cooking spray to grease the surface.

Scoop Batter onto the Griddle:
- Using a 1/4 cup measuring cup, scoop the pancake batter onto the preheated griddle. Spread the batter slightly to form a round pancake.

Cook until Bubbles Form:
- Cook the pancakes until bubbles form on the surface, and the edges begin to look set. This usually takes about 2-3 minutes.

Flip and Cook the Other Side:

- Flip the pancakes and cook the other side until golden brown, usually for an additional 1-2 minutes.

Repeat:
- Repeat the process with the remaining batter.

Serve:
- Serve the Blueberry and Ricotta Pancakes warm, and optionally, top with additional blueberries, maple syrup, or a dollop of ricotta.

Enjoy these flavorful and fluffy pancakes as a delightful breakfast or brunch treat! The combination of ricotta and blueberries creates a creamy and sweet texture that is sure to be a crowd-pleaser.

Blueberry Basil Lemonade

Ingredients:

- 1 cup fresh or frozen blueberries
- 1/2 cup fresh basil leaves, loosely packed
- 1 cup freshly squeezed lemon juice (about 4-6 lemons)
- 1 cup granulated sugar (adjust to taste)
- 5 cups cold water
- Ice cubes
- Lemon slices and basil leaves for garnish (optional)

Instructions:

Prepare Blueberry Basil Syrup:
- In a small saucepan, combine the blueberries, basil leaves, and 1 cup of water. Bring to a simmer over medium heat, then reduce the heat to low and let it simmer for about 5-7 minutes.
- Using a spoon, mash the blueberries and basil to release their flavors. Allow the mixture to cool for a few minutes.
- Strain the blueberry basil mixture through a fine mesh sieve or cheesecloth into a bowl, pressing down to extract as much liquid as possible. Discard the solids.

Make Lemonade Base:
- In a large pitcher, combine the freshly squeezed lemon juice and granulated sugar. Stir until the sugar is dissolved.

Combine Ingredients:
- Pour the strained blueberry basil syrup into the pitcher with the lemonade base.
- Add the remaining 4 cups of cold water to the pitcher and mix well.

Chill:
- Place the pitcher in the refrigerator to chill for at least 1-2 hours.

Serve:
- When ready to serve, fill glasses with ice cubes and pour the Blueberry Basil Lemonade over the ice.

Garnish (Optional):
- Garnish each glass with a slice of lemon and a fresh basil leaf for an extra touch of flavor and presentation.

Enjoy:

- Stir before drinking and enjoy the refreshing and vibrant Blueberry Basil Lemonade.

This homemade lemonade is perfect for hot summer days, picnics, or any occasion where you want a burst of fruity and herbal goodness in your drink.

Blueberry Cinnamon Rolls

Ingredients:

For the Dough:

- 1 cup warm milk (110°F/43°C)
- 2 1/4 teaspoons (1 packet) active dry yeast
- 1/4 cup granulated sugar
- 1/3 cup unsalted butter, melted
- 1 teaspoon vanilla extract
- 1 teaspoon salt
- 3 to 3 1/2 cups all-purpose flour

For the Filling:

- 1/2 cup unsalted butter, softened
- 1 cup brown sugar, packed
- 2 tablespoons ground cinnamon
- 1 1/2 cups fresh blueberries

For the Cream Cheese Frosting:

- 4 ounces cream cheese, softened
- 1/4 cup unsalted butter, softened
- 1 cup powdered sugar
- 1/2 teaspoon vanilla extract

Instructions:

Prepare the Dough:
- In a bowl, combine the warm milk and yeast. Let it sit for 5 minutes until frothy.
- Add sugar, melted butter, vanilla extract, and salt to the yeast mixture. Stir to combine.
- Gradually add the flour, one cup at a time, until a soft dough forms. Knead the dough on a floured surface for about 5 minutes until smooth and elastic.
- Place the dough in a greased bowl, cover with a damp cloth, and let it rise in a warm place for 1-2 hours or until doubled in size.

Prepare the Filling:
- In a small bowl, mix together the softened butter, brown sugar, and ground cinnamon to create the filling.
- Roll out the dough on a floured surface into a 12x18-inch rectangle.
- Spread the filling mixture evenly over the rolled-out dough, leaving a small border around the edges. Sprinkle fresh blueberries over the filling.

Roll and Cut:
- Starting from the long edge, tightly roll the dough into a log. Pinch the seam to seal.
- Using a sharp knife, cut the log into 12 equal slices.

Place in Pan and Rise:
- Place the slices in a greased baking pan, leaving a little space between each roll. Cover the pan with a damp cloth and let the rolls rise for another 30-45 minutes.

Preheat Oven:
- Preheat your oven to 375°F (190°C).

Bake:
- Bake the blueberry cinnamon rolls for 20-25 minutes or until golden brown.

Prepare the Frosting:
- While the rolls are baking, prepare the cream cheese frosting. In a bowl, beat together the softened cream cheese, softened butter, powdered sugar, and vanilla extract until smooth.

Frost the Rolls:
- Once the rolls are out of the oven and slightly cooled, spread the cream cheese frosting over the warm rolls.

Serve:
- Serve the Blueberry Cinnamon Rolls warm and enjoy the gooey, fruity, and delicious treat!

These Blueberry Cinnamon Rolls are a delightful breakfast or brunch option, combining the classic cinnamon roll flavor with the sweetness of fresh blueberries.

Blueberry Crumble Bars

Ingredients:

For the Crust and Crumble:

- 1 cup unsalted butter, softened
- 1/2 cup granulated sugar
- 1 teaspoon vanilla extract
- 2 cups all-purpose flour
- 1/2 teaspoon baking powder
- 1/4 teaspoon salt

For the Blueberry Filling:

- 3 cups fresh or frozen blueberries
- 1/2 cup granulated sugar
- 2 tablespoons lemon juice
- 1 tablespoon cornstarch

Instructions:

Preheat the Oven:
- Preheat your oven to 375°F (190°C). Grease a 9x13-inch baking pan or line it with parchment paper.

Prepare the Crust and Crumble:
- In a large mixing bowl, cream together the softened butter, granulated sugar, and vanilla extract until light and fluffy.
- In a separate bowl, whisk together the flour, baking powder, and salt. Gradually add the dry ingredients to the butter mixture, mixing until a crumbly dough forms.

Press into Pan:
- Press about two-thirds of the crumbly dough into the bottom of the prepared baking pan, creating an even crust.

Prepare the Blueberry Filling:
- In a saucepan, combine the blueberries, granulated sugar, lemon juice, and cornstarch. Cook over medium heat, stirring constantly until the mixture

- thickens and the blueberries release their juices. This usually takes about 5-7 minutes.
- Remove the blueberry filling from heat and let it cool slightly.

Layer Blueberry Filling:
- Spread the blueberry filling evenly over the crust in the baking pan.

Crumble Topping:
- Take the remaining crumbly dough and sprinkle it evenly over the blueberry filling, creating a crumbly topping.

Bake:
- Bake in the preheated oven for 35-40 minutes or until the top is golden brown.

Cool:
- Allow the blueberry crumble bars to cool completely in the pan before cutting into squares.

Serve:
- Once cooled, cut into bars and serve. Optionally, dust with powdered sugar before serving.

These Blueberry Crumble Bars are a delightful combination of buttery crust, sweet blueberry filling, and crumbly topping. They make for a perfect treat for dessert or as a snack with a cup of coffee or tea. Enjoy!

Blueberry and Feta Stuffed Chicken Breast

Ingredients:

- 4 boneless, skinless chicken breasts
- Salt and black pepper to taste
- 1 cup fresh blueberries
- 1/2 cup crumbled feta cheese
- 2 tablespoons fresh basil, chopped
- 1 tablespoon balsamic glaze (optional)
- Olive oil for cooking

Instructions:

Preheat the Oven:
- Preheat your oven to 375°F (190°C).

Prepare Chicken Breasts:
- Place each chicken breast between two sheets of plastic wrap and pound them to an even thickness using a meat mallet. Season both sides with salt and black pepper.

Make the Blueberry and Feta Filling:
- In a bowl, mix together the fresh blueberries, crumbled feta cheese, and chopped fresh basil.

Stuff the Chicken Breasts:
- Cut a slit horizontally into the side of each chicken breast to create a pocket without cutting all the way through.
- Stuff each chicken breast with the blueberry and feta mixture, pressing down to secure the filling.

Secure with Toothpicks (Optional):
- If needed, secure the opening with toothpicks to keep the filling from falling out during cooking.

Season and Sear:
- Season the outside of the chicken breasts with a bit more salt and pepper.
- In an oven-safe skillet, heat olive oil over medium-high heat. Sear the chicken breasts for about 2-3 minutes per side until they develop a golden-brown crust.

Finish in the Oven:
- If using an oven-safe skillet, transfer it to the preheated oven. Alternatively, transfer the seared chicken breasts to a baking dish.

- Bake in the oven for 20-25 minutes or until the chicken is cooked through and reaches an internal temperature of 165°F (74°C).

Baste with Balsamic Glaze (Optional):
- If desired, drizzle balsamic glaze over the chicken during the last 5 minutes of baking for extra flavor.

Rest and Serve:
- Allow the chicken to rest for a few minutes before serving. Remove any toothpicks before serving.

Serve:
- Serve the Blueberry and Feta Stuffed Chicken Breast with your favorite side dishes.

This dish offers a delightful combination of sweet and savory flavors, making it a unique and delicious option for a special dinner. The blueberries and feta add a burst of freshness and richness to the chicken.

Blueberry Whipped Cream

Ingredients:

- 1 cup heavy whipping cream, chilled
- 1/4 cup powdered sugar (adjust to taste)
- 1/2 cup fresh blueberries
- 1/2 teaspoon vanilla extract

Instructions:

Chill Mixing Bowl and Whisk:
- Place your mixing bowl and whisk (or beaters) in the refrigerator for about 15 minutes to chill.

Prepare Blueberries:
- In a blender or food processor, puree the fresh blueberries until smooth. You can strain the mixture to remove seeds if desired, but keeping some blueberry bits can add texture.

Whip the Cream:
- Pour the chilled heavy whipping cream into the chilled mixing bowl. Begin whipping the cream on medium speed.
- As the cream starts to thicken, gradually add the powdered sugar and continue whipping.
- Add the vanilla extract.

Incorporate Blueberry Puree:
- Once the whipped cream reaches stiff peaks, gently fold in the blueberry puree. Be careful not to overmix; you want to create a swirled effect.

Taste and Adjust:
- Taste the blueberry whipped cream and adjust the sweetness by adding more powdered sugar if necessary.

Serve:
- Use the blueberry whipped cream immediately or cover and refrigerate until ready to use.

Enjoy:
- Serve the Blueberry Whipped Cream on top of desserts, pancakes, waffles, or any other treats where whipped cream is desired.

This Blueberry Whipped Cream adds a burst of fruity flavor and a beautiful purple hue to your desserts. It's a perfect complement to a wide range of sweets and can elevate the overall taste experience.

Blueberry and Peach Sangria

Ingredients:

- 1 bottle of white wine (750 ml), such as Sauvignon Blanc or Pinot Grigio
- 1/2 cup peach schnapps or peach liqueur
- 1/4 cup brandy
- 1/4 cup simple syrup (adjust to taste)
- 1 cup blueberries
- 2 peaches, sliced
- 1 lemon, sliced
- 2 cups sparkling water or club soda
- Ice cubes

Instructions:

Prepare Fruits:
- Wash and slice the peaches and lemon. Rinse the blueberries.

Make Simple Syrup:
- In a small saucepan, combine equal parts water and sugar. Heat over medium heat, stirring until the sugar dissolves. Allow the simple syrup to cool.

Mix Sangria:
- In a large pitcher, combine the white wine, peach schnapps, brandy, and cooled simple syrup. Stir well to mix the ingredients.

Add Fruits:
- Add the sliced peaches, blueberries, and lemon slices to the pitcher. Stir gently to combine.

Chill:
- Place the pitcher in the refrigerator and let the sangria chill for at least 2-4 hours, allowing the flavors to meld. For an even more intense flavor, you can leave it in the refrigerator overnight.

Add Sparkling Water:
- Just before serving, add the sparkling water or club soda to the sangria. Stir gently to combine.

Serve:
- Fill glasses with ice cubes and pour the Blueberry and Peach Sangria over the ice.

Garnish (Optional):
- Garnish each glass with additional blueberries, peach slices, or lemon slices if desired.

Enjoy:
- Sip and enjoy the refreshing and fruity goodness of Blueberry and Peach Sangria.

This sangria is perfect for outdoor gatherings, picnics, or any summer celebration. The combination of blueberries and peaches adds a sweet and vibrant touch to the classic white wine sangria. Cheers!

Blueberry Oatmeal Cookies

Ingredients:

- 1 cup unsalted butter, softened
- 1 cup granulated sugar
- 2 large eggs
- 1 teaspoon vanilla extract
- 2 cups old-fashioned oats
- 1 1/2 cups all-purpose flour
- 1/2 teaspoon baking soda
- 1/2 teaspoon cinnamon
- 1/4 teaspoon salt
- 1 cup fresh or frozen blueberries

Instructions:

Preheat the Oven:
- Preheat your oven to 350°F (175°C). Line baking sheets with parchment paper.

Cream Butter and Sugar:
- In a large bowl, cream together the softened butter and granulated sugar until light and fluffy.

Add Eggs and Vanilla:
- Add the eggs one at a time, beating well after each addition. Stir in the vanilla extract.

Combine Dry Ingredients:
- In a separate bowl, whisk together the oats, all-purpose flour, baking soda, cinnamon, and salt.

Add Dry Ingredients to Wet Ingredients:
- Gradually add the dry ingredients to the wet ingredients, mixing until just combined.

Fold in Blueberries:
- Gently fold in the blueberries until evenly distributed throughout the cookie dough.

Scoop and Bake:
- Drop rounded tablespoons of dough onto the prepared baking sheets, spacing them about 2 inches apart.

Bake:

- Bake in the preheated oven for 12-15 minutes or until the edges are golden brown.

Cool:
- Allow the cookies to cool on the baking sheets for a few minutes before transferring them to wire racks to cool completely.

Serve:
- Once the Blueberry Oatmeal Cookies are completely cooled, serve and enjoy!

These cookies are chewy, hearty, and bursting with the sweetness of blueberries. They make for a delicious treat for breakfast, snack time, or dessert. Feel free to add nuts or white chocolate chips if you desire additional flavor and texture.

Blueberry and Lemon Sorbet

Ingredients:

- 3 cups fresh or frozen blueberries
- 1 cup granulated sugar
- 1 cup water
- Zest and juice of 2 lemons

Instructions:

Make Simple Syrup:
- In a saucepan, combine the granulated sugar and water. Heat over medium heat, stirring until the sugar completely dissolves. Allow the mixture to cool to room temperature. This is your simple syrup.

Prepare Blueberries:
- If using fresh blueberries, rinse them under cold water. If using frozen blueberries, allow them to thaw slightly.

Blend Blueberries:
- In a blender or food processor, puree the blueberries until smooth.

Strain Blueberry Puree (Optional):
- If you prefer a smoother sorbet, you can strain the blueberry puree through a fine mesh sieve to remove the seeds. Press down with a spatula to extract as much liquid as possible.

Combine Ingredients:
- In a bowl, combine the blueberry puree, simple syrup, lemon zest, and lemon juice. Mix well to ensure all ingredients are thoroughly combined.

Chill Mixture:
- Place the mixture in the refrigerator for at least 2 hours or until it is well chilled.

Freeze in Ice Cream Maker:
- Transfer the chilled mixture to an ice cream maker and churn according to the manufacturer's instructions until you achieve a sorbet-like consistency.

Transfer to Freezer Container:
- Transfer the sorbet to a lidded freezer-safe container.

Freeze:
- Freeze the sorbet for an additional 2-4 hours or until it reaches your desired firmness.

Serve:

- Scoop the Blueberry and Lemon Sorbet into bowls or cones, and enjoy!

This sorbet is a delightful and guilt-free dessert, perfect for hot summer days or any time you crave a refreshing and fruity treat. The combination of blueberries and lemon creates a harmonious balance of sweetness and tartness.

Blueberry and Walnut Bread

Ingredients:

- 2 cups all-purpose flour
- 1 teaspoon baking powder
- 1/2 teaspoon baking soda
- 1/4 teaspoon salt
- 1/2 cup unsalted butter, softened
- 1 cup granulated sugar
- 2 large eggs
- 1 teaspoon vanilla extract
- 1 cup fresh blueberries
- 1/2 cup chopped walnuts
- 1 cup buttermilk

Instructions:

Preheat the Oven:
- Preheat your oven to 350°F (175°C). Grease and flour a 9x5-inch loaf pan.

Prepare Dry Ingredients:
- In a medium bowl, whisk together the all-purpose flour, baking powder, baking soda, and salt. Set aside.

Cream Butter and Sugar:
- In a large bowl, cream together the softened butter and granulated sugar until light and fluffy.

Add Eggs and Vanilla:
- Add the eggs one at a time, beating well after each addition. Stir in the vanilla extract.

Combine Wet and Dry Ingredients:
- Gradually add the dry ingredients to the wet ingredients, mixing just until combined.

Add Buttermilk:
- Stir in the buttermilk until the batter is smooth.

Fold in Blueberries and Walnuts:
- Gently fold in the fresh blueberries and chopped walnuts until evenly distributed throughout the batter.

Pour into Loaf Pan:

- Pour the batter into the prepared loaf pan, spreading it evenly.

Bake:
- Bake in the preheated oven for 55-65 minutes or until a toothpick inserted into the center comes out clean or with just a few moist crumbs.

Cool:
- Allow the Blueberry and Walnut Bread to cool in the pan for about 15 minutes, then transfer it to a wire rack to cool completely.

Slice and Serve:
- Once cooled, slice the bread and serve. Enjoy it as is or with a spread of butter or cream cheese.

This Blueberry and Walnut Bread is perfect for breakfast or as a sweet treat any time of the day. The combination of juicy blueberries and crunchy walnuts adds a delightful texture and flavor to the moist bread.

Blueberry and Cream Cheese Stuffed French Toast Casserole

Ingredients:

For the French Toast Casserole:

- 1 loaf of French bread, cut into 1-inch cubes
- 1 cup fresh or frozen blueberries
- 8 ounces cream cheese, softened
- 8 large eggs
- 2 cups milk
- 1/2 cup heavy cream
- 1/2 cup granulated sugar
- 2 teaspoons vanilla extract
- 1/2 teaspoon ground cinnamon
- Pinch of salt

For the Streusel Topping:

- 1/2 cup all-purpose flour
- 1/2 cup brown sugar, packed
- 1/4 cup cold unsalted butter, cut into small pieces
- 1/2 teaspoon ground cinnamon
- 1/4 cup chopped nuts (such as pecans or walnuts, optional)

For Serving:

- Maple syrup
- Powdered sugar (optional)

Instructions:

Prepare the Cream Cheese Filling:
- In a bowl, beat the softened cream cheese until smooth.

Prepare the French Toast Mixture:
- In a large mixing bowl, whisk together the eggs, milk, heavy cream, granulated sugar, vanilla extract, ground cinnamon, and a pinch of salt.

Assemble the Casserole:
- Grease a 9x13-inch baking dish. Place half of the cubed French bread in the dish. Dot the cream cheese over the bread, and sprinkle the blueberries evenly.
- Top with the remaining bread cubes.
- Pour the egg mixture over the bread, ensuring all pieces are well-coated. Press down slightly to help the bread absorb the liquid.

Prepare the Streusel Topping:
- In a small bowl, combine the flour, brown sugar, cold butter pieces, ground cinnamon, and chopped nuts (if using). Use a fork or your fingers to crumble the mixture until it resembles coarse crumbs.

Add Streusel Topping:
- Sprinkle the streusel topping evenly over the French toast casserole.

Cover and Refrigerate:
- Cover the baking dish with plastic wrap and refrigerate for at least 4 hours or overnight. This allows the bread to absorb the liquid and the flavors to meld.

Preheat Oven:
- Preheat your oven to 350°F (175°C).

Bake:
- Bake the casserole, uncovered, for 45-55 minutes or until the top is golden brown and the center is set.

Serve:
- Allow the casserole to cool for a few minutes before slicing. Serve with maple syrup and a dusting of powdered sugar if desired.

This Blueberry and Cream Cheese Stuffed French Toast Casserole is a delightful combination of creamy, fruity, and sweet flavors. It's perfect for special occasions or weekend brunch gatherings.

Blueberry and Pecan Quinoa Salad

Ingredients:

For the Quinoa:

- 1 cup quinoa, rinsed
- 2 cups water
- 1/2 teaspoon salt

For the Salad:

- 1 cup fresh blueberries
- 1/2 cup pecans, toasted and chopped
- 1/2 cup crumbled feta cheese (optional)
- 1/4 cup red onion, finely chopped
- 1/4 cup fresh mint leaves, chopped

For the Dressing:

- 3 tablespoons extra-virgin olive oil
- 2 tablespoons balsamic vinegar
- 1 tablespoon honey
- Salt and black pepper to taste

Instructions:

Cook the Quinoa:
- In a medium saucepan, combine the quinoa, water, and salt. Bring to a boil, then reduce the heat to low, cover, and simmer for 15-20 minutes or until the quinoa is cooked and water is absorbed.
- Once cooked, fluff the quinoa with a fork and let it cool to room temperature.

Prepare the Dressing:
- In a small bowl, whisk together the extra-virgin olive oil, balsamic vinegar, honey, salt, and black pepper to create the dressing. Adjust the sweetness and acidity to your taste.

Assemble the Salad:

- In a large salad bowl, combine the cooled quinoa, fresh blueberries, toasted and chopped pecans, crumbled feta cheese (if using), chopped red onion, and fresh mint leaves.

Add Dressing:
- Drizzle the dressing over the salad ingredients. Toss the salad gently to coat everything evenly with the dressing.

Chill (Optional):
- If you prefer a chilled salad, refrigerate for about 30 minutes before serving.

Serve:
- Serve the Blueberry and Pecan Quinoa Salad as a refreshing and nutritious side dish or a light meal.

Optional Additions:
- Feel free to customize the salad by adding other ingredients such as baby spinach, arugula, or crumbled goat cheese.

This Blueberry and Pecan Quinoa Salad is a perfect blend of textures and flavors, making it a delicious and wholesome choice for lunch or as a side dish for dinner. Enjoy the nutty crunch of pecans, the sweetness of blueberries, and the protein-packed quinoa in every bite.

Blueberry and Nutella Crepes

Ingredients:

For the Crepes:

- 1 cup all-purpose flour
- 2 large eggs
- 1 cup milk
- 1/2 cup water
- 2 tablespoons melted butter
- 1 tablespoon sugar
- 1/2 teaspoon vanilla extract
- Pinch of salt

For Filling:

- Nutella (as much as desired)
- Fresh blueberries

Optional Toppings:

- Powdered sugar
- Whipped cream
- Sliced bananas
- Chopped nuts

Instructions:

Prepare Crepe Batter:
- In a blender, combine the flour, eggs, milk, water, melted butter, sugar, vanilla extract, and a pinch of salt. Blend until smooth. Let the batter rest in the refrigerator for at least 30 minutes to allow any bubbles to settle.

Cook Crepes:
- Heat a non-stick skillet or crepe pan over medium heat. Lightly grease the pan with butter or cooking spray.

- Pour about 1/4 cup of batter into the center of the pan and quickly swirl it around to spread the batter thinly. Cook for about 1-2 minutes or until the edges start to lift.
- Flip the crepe and cook for an additional 30 seconds to 1 minute on the other side. Repeat until all the batter is used.

Spread Nutella:
- Lay each crepe flat on a plate. Spread a generous layer of Nutella over the surface of each crepe.

Add Blueberries:
- Sprinkle fresh blueberries over the Nutella layer.

Fold Crepes:
- Fold the crepes in half and then in half again to create a triangle shape.

Serve:
- Place the Blueberry and Nutella Crepes on serving plates. Optionally, top with additional blueberries, a dusting of powdered sugar, a dollop of whipped cream, or chopped nuts.

Enjoy:
- Serve immediately and enjoy the delicious combination of warm crepes, creamy Nutella, and juicy blueberries.

These Blueberry and Nutella Crepes make for a delightful dessert or special breakfast. The contrast between the rich Nutella and the burst of freshness from blueberries creates a perfect harmony of flavors. Customize the toppings according to your preference for an extra special treat.

Blueberry Basil Chicken

Ingredients:

- 4 boneless, skinless chicken breasts
- Salt and black pepper to taste
- 1 tablespoon olive oil
- 1/2 cup diced red onion
- 2 cloves garlic, minced
- 1 cup fresh or frozen blueberries
- 2 tablespoons balsamic vinegar
- 1 tablespoon honey
- 1/4 cup fresh basil leaves, chopped
- 1/2 cup chicken broth

Instructions:

Season Chicken:
- Season the chicken breasts with salt and black pepper on both sides.

Sear Chicken:
- In a large skillet, heat olive oil over medium-high heat. Add the chicken breasts and sear them for about 3-4 minutes per side or until golden brown. Remove the chicken from the skillet and set aside.

Saute Onion and Garlic:
- In the same skillet, add diced red onion and minced garlic. Saute for 2-3 minutes or until the onion becomes translucent.

Prepare Blueberry Basil Sauce:
- Add fresh or frozen blueberries to the skillet and cook for another 2 minutes until the blueberries start to release their juices.
- Pour in balsamic vinegar, honey, and chicken broth. Stir to combine.
- Add chopped fresh basil to the skillet and mix well. Let the sauce simmer for a few minutes to allow the flavors to meld.

Return Chicken to Skillet:
- Return the seared chicken breasts to the skillet, nestling them into the blueberry basil sauce.

Simmer:
- Reduce the heat to low and let the chicken simmer in the sauce for 10-15 minutes or until the chicken is cooked through and the sauce has thickened.

Serve:
- Serve the Blueberry Basil Chicken over rice, quinoa, or your preferred side dish. Spoon some of the blueberry basil sauce over the chicken before serving.

Garnish (Optional):
- Garnish with additional fresh basil leaves for a burst of color and added freshness.

Enjoy:
- Enjoy this unique and flavorful Blueberry Basil Chicken dish!

The combination of sweet blueberries and aromatic basil creates a deliciously different flavor profile for chicken. This dish is perfect for a special dinner and will surely impress with its vibrant colors and enticing taste.

Blueberry Pistachio Energy Bites

Ingredients:

- 1 cup rolled oats
- 1/2 cup dried blueberries
- 1/2 cup shelled pistachios
- 1/2 cup almond butter (or any nut or seed butter of your choice)
- 1/4 cup honey or maple syrup
- 1 teaspoon vanilla extract
- Pinch of salt (optional)
- Additional ingredients for coating (e.g., shredded coconut, crushed pistachios)

Instructions:

Prepare Ingredients:
- If your pistachios are not already shelled, remove the shells to get the green pistachio kernels.

Combine Dry Ingredients:
- In a food processor, combine rolled oats, dried blueberries, and shelled pistachios. Pulse the mixture until it forms a coarse, crumbly texture.

Add Wet Ingredients:
- Add almond butter, honey or maple syrup, vanilla extract, and a pinch of salt (if using) to the food processor.

Blend:
- Process the mixture until it comes together into a sticky dough-like consistency.

Form Energy Bites:
- Scoop out small portions of the mixture and roll them between your hands to form bite-sized balls. If the mixture is too sticky, you can wet your hands with a bit of water to make it easier.

Coat the Energy Bites:
- Optional: Roll the energy bites in additional ingredients for coating, such as shredded coconut or crushed pistachios.

Chill:
- Place the formed energy bites on a parchment-lined tray and chill in the refrigerator for at least 30 minutes to help them set.

Store:

- Once the Blueberry Pistachio Energy Bites are firm, transfer them to an airtight container. Store in the refrigerator for freshness.

Enjoy:
- Enjoy these energy bites as a quick and healthy snack whenever you need a boost of energy.

These Blueberry Pistachio Energy Bites are not only delicious but also packed with nutrient-dense ingredients. They make for a convenient and satisfying snack for a busy day or a pre-workout pick-me-up.

Blueberry and Spinach Stuffed Salmon

Ingredients:

- 4 salmon fillets
- Salt and black pepper to taste
- 2 cups fresh baby spinach, chopped
- 1/2 cup fresh blueberries
- 1/4 cup feta cheese, crumbled
- 2 tablespoons balsamic glaze
- 2 tablespoons olive oil
- 2 cloves garlic, minced
- 1 teaspoon dried thyme or 1 tablespoon fresh thyme leaves

Instructions:

Preheat the Oven:
- Preheat your oven to 375°F (190°C).

Prepare the Spinach and Blueberry Mixture:
- In a bowl, combine the chopped baby spinach, fresh blueberries, crumbled feta cheese, minced garlic, and thyme. Mix well to create the stuffing.

Prepare the Salmon:
- Lay the salmon fillets on a cutting board. Using a sharp knife, make a horizontal cut along the side of each fillet to create a pocket for the stuffing. Be careful not to cut all the way through.

Season Salmon:
- Season the salmon fillets with salt and black pepper, both inside the pocket and on the outside.

Stuff Salmon:
- Stuff each salmon fillet with the spinach and blueberry mixture, pressing the stuffing gently into the pocket.

Secure with Toothpicks (Optional):
- If needed, secure the opening of the salmon pockets with toothpicks to hold the stuffing in place.

Arrange in Baking Dish:
- Place the stuffed salmon fillets in a baking dish.

Drizzle with Olive Oil and Balsamic Glaze:
- Drizzle the olive oil and balsamic glaze over the stuffed salmon fillets.

Bake:

- Bake in the preheated oven for 15-20 minutes or until the salmon is cooked through and flakes easily with a fork.

Serve:
- Remove the toothpicks if used and serve the Blueberry and Spinach Stuffed Salmon hot. Optionally, drizzle with additional balsamic glaze before serving.

This Blueberry and Spinach Stuffed Salmon is a delicious and elegant dish that pairs well with a variety of side dishes. The combination of the savory salmon, sweet blueberries, and earthy spinach creates a delightful harmony of flavors.

Blueberry and Balsamic Bruschetta

Ingredients:

- Baguette or French bread, sliced
- 1 cup fresh blueberries
- 1/4 cup fresh basil leaves, chopped
- 1/4 cup red onion, finely chopped
- 2 tablespoons balsamic glaze
- 2 tablespoons extra-virgin olive oil
- 1 teaspoon honey
- Salt and black pepper to taste
- Optional: Goat cheese or feta cheese for spreading

Instructions:

Preheat the Oven:
- Preheat your oven to 375°F (190°C).

Toast the Bread:
- Place the sliced baguette or French bread on a baking sheet. Toast in the preheated oven for 5-7 minutes or until the edges are golden brown.

Prepare Blueberry Mixture:
- In a bowl, combine fresh blueberries, chopped basil leaves, and finely chopped red onion.

Make Balsamic Dressing:
- In a small bowl, whisk together balsamic glaze, extra-virgin olive oil, honey, salt, and black pepper to create the dressing.

Combine and Toss:
- Pour the balsamic dressing over the blueberry mixture. Gently toss to coat the ingredients evenly.

Assemble Bruschetta:
- Optional: Spread a layer of goat cheese or feta cheese on each toasted bread slice.
- Spoon the blueberry and balsamic mixture over the cheese-covered or plain toasted bread slices.

Drizzle Extra Balsamic Glaze:
- Drizzle a little extra balsamic glaze over the top of each bruschetta for added flavor.

Serve:

- Arrange the Blueberry and Balsamic Bruschetta on a serving platter and serve immediately.

This appetizer offers a perfect balance of sweet, savory, and tangy flavors. The juicy blueberries, fresh basil, and balsamic glaze create a colorful and delightful topping for the crispy bread. It's a great addition to any gathering or as a light and sophisticated snack.

Blueberry Tiramisu

Ingredients:

For the Blueberry Sauce:

- 2 cups fresh or frozen blueberries
- 1/4 cup granulated sugar
- 1 tablespoon lemon juice

For the Tiramisu:

- 1 cup heavy cream
- 1 cup mascarpone cheese
- 1/2 cup powdered sugar
- 1 teaspoon vanilla extract
- 1 cup blueberry sauce (from the above ingredients)
- Ladyfingers (enough to cover the base of your serving dish)
- Fresh blueberries for garnish
- Cocoa powder for dusting (optional)

Instructions:

For the Blueberry Sauce:

Cook Blueberries:
- In a saucepan, combine blueberries, granulated sugar, and lemon juice. Cook over medium heat, stirring occasionally, until the blueberries break down and the mixture thickens. This usually takes about 10-15 minutes.

Cool:
- Allow the blueberry sauce to cool to room temperature. You can also refrigerate it until ready to use.

For the Tiramisu:

Whip the Cream:
- In a mixing bowl, whip the heavy cream until stiff peaks form.

Prepare Mascarpone Mixture:
- In another bowl, whisk together mascarpone cheese, powdered sugar, and vanilla extract until smooth.

Combine Cream and Mascarpone Mixture:
- Gently fold the whipped cream into the mascarpone mixture until well combined.

Layer the Tiramisu:
- In your serving dish, start by placing a layer of ladyfingers at the bottom.
- Spread a layer of the mascarpone and cream mixture over the ladyfingers.
- Spoon a layer of the blueberry sauce over the cream mixture.
- Repeat the layers until you reach the top of the dish, finishing with a layer of the mascarpone and cream mixture.

Chill:
- Cover the Blueberry Tiramisu with plastic wrap and refrigerate for at least 4 hours or overnight to allow the flavors to meld and the dessert to set.

Garnish and Serve:
- Before serving, garnish the top with fresh blueberries and dust with cocoa powder if desired.

Enjoy:
- Slice and serve the Blueberry Tiramisu chilled.

This Blueberry Tiramisu offers a fruity and luscious variation to the classic dessert. The combination of creamy mascarpone, sweet blueberry sauce, and delicate ladyfingers creates a delightful treat that's perfect for special occasions or as a refreshing dessert on a warm day.

www.ingramcontent.com/pod-product-compliance
Lightning Source LLC
LaVergne TN
LVHW061944070526
838199LV00060B/3966